Hues of Africa

This Book Belongs to:

Journey Between the Lines

© 2021 Tiffany Heard. All rights reserved.

This book or parts thereof may not be reproduced in any form, stored in any retrieval system, or transmitted in any form by any means—electronic, mechanical, photocopy, recording, or otherwise—without prior written permission of the publisher, except as provided by United States of America copyright law.

ISBN: 978-1-7370011-1-9

Dedication

I would like to dedicate this book to my grandmother Margaret Vaughn who was affectionately known as my twin. Growing up as a child, I would watch her complete numerous activity books. Although she is no longer here to stroke her colored pencils across the page, solve the brainstorming puzzles or take the long journey to Africa, I know she would be proud of my accomplishments thus far. May she rest in heaven as her light continues to shine through me.

Truth about Africa

Fill in the blanks by finding the term in the word search puzzle.

There are 54 _____ in Africa.

Africa is the second largest _____.

The 2 main religions are _____ and Christians.

_____ is the hottest country and has its own alphabet.

The _____ river is the largest river and spreads across 11 countries.

Africa is rich in natural resources and produces both gold and _____.

Ethiopia and _____ were the only 2 countries in Africa not colonized by foreigners.

The University of Sankore is the oldest university in Africa and can be found in _____ Mali.

The tallest animal is the giraffe, largest animal is the African elephant & the deadliest is the _____.

There are approximately 2,000 languages with different dialects but _____ is the most widely spoken.

Africa is the "cradle of humankind," _____ found here shows that humans evolved 10 million years prior and spread from the continent.

C	V	F	W	F	P	X	Y	Q	E
A	O	U	O	B	D	Q	C	K	T
R	G	U	T	S	O	P	P	I	H
A	H	J	N	K	S	W	M	L	I
B	E	Y	Z	T	U	I	X	R	O
I	S	L	A	M	R	B	L	Z	P
C	E	L	I	N	G	I	M	S	I
L	I	B	E	R	I	A	E	I	A
D	I	A	M	O	N	D	S	S	T
V	T	N	E	N	I	T	N	O	C

Hues of Africa: Journey Between the Lines

By: Tiffany Heard

African Cuisine

Below is a group of food that belongs to certain cardinal direction in African (South, North, West, East). Please write S, N, W or E in the square to identify the correct answer.

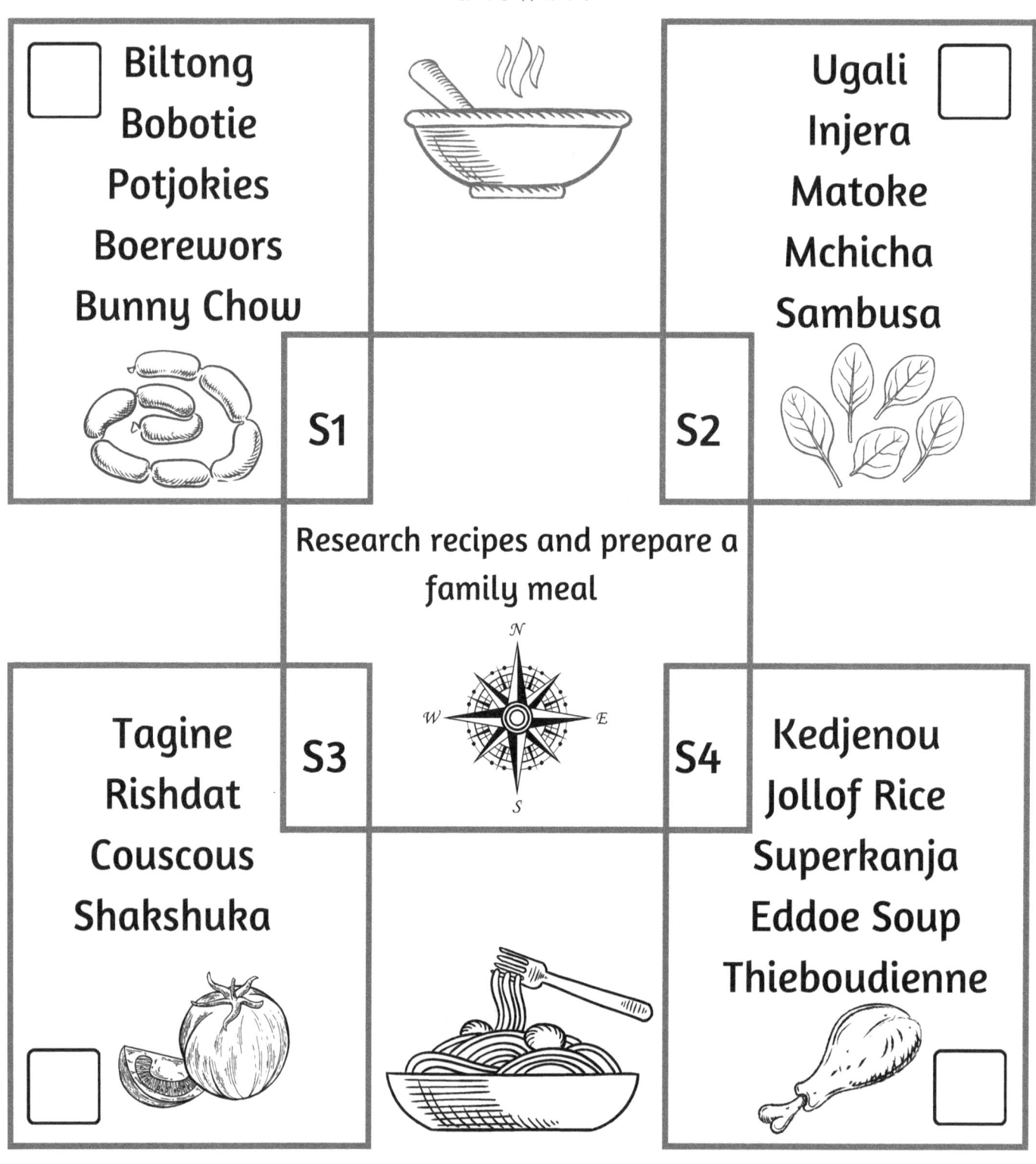

Box 1 (S1):
- Biltong
- Bobotie
- Potjokies
- Boerewors
- Bunny Chow

Box 2 (S2):
- Ugali
- Injera
- Matoke
- Mchicha
- Sambusa

Research recipes and prepare a family meal

Box 3 (S3):
- Tagine
- Rishdat
- Couscous
- Shakshuka

Box 4 (S4):
- Kedjenou
- Jollof Rice
- Superkanja
- Eddoe Soup
- Thieboudienne

AFRICAN FABRIC

DRAW A LINE AND MATCH THE STATEMENT TO THE FABRIC GRAPHIC

ADINKRA CLOTH ORIGINATED IN GHANA. IT IS MADE BY EMBROIDERING DYED COTTON AND STAMPING IT WITH VARIOUS CALABASH SYMBOLS. ADINKRA MEANS FAREWELL AND IS USED AT FUNERALS. BROWN & BLACK ARE ASSOCIATED WITH DEATH. WHITE, YELLOW & LIGHT BLUE ARE MORE FESTIVE.

KENTE CLOTH COMES FROM THE ASHANTI PEOPLE IN GHANA AND WAS USED TO DRESS THE KING AND ROYAL COURT. MOST KENTE WEAVERS ARE MEN. KENTE IS WOVEN ON A HORIZONTAL LOOM AND IT INVOLVES PARALLEL THREADS OF WARP, WERP AND TREADLES.

MUD CLOTH ORIGINATED IN MALI AND IS CALLED BOGOLANFINI. THE HANDWOVEN COTTON IS STITCHED TOGETHER WITH PATTERNS AND NATURAL DYES INCLUDING AGED RIVER MUD. TYPICAL COLORS INCLUDE WHITE, YELLOW, PURPLE, BEIGE, RICH BROWN AND RUST.

BATIK IS MADE BY APPLYING VARIOUS PATTERNS OF MELTED WAX ON THE FABRIC. THE WAX IS REMOVED BY BOILING THE CLOTH. COMMON DYE COLORS INCLUDE INDIGO, BLUE, YELLOW, GREEN, BROWN AND PURPLE..

Activity: Color each flag and write the name of the country below

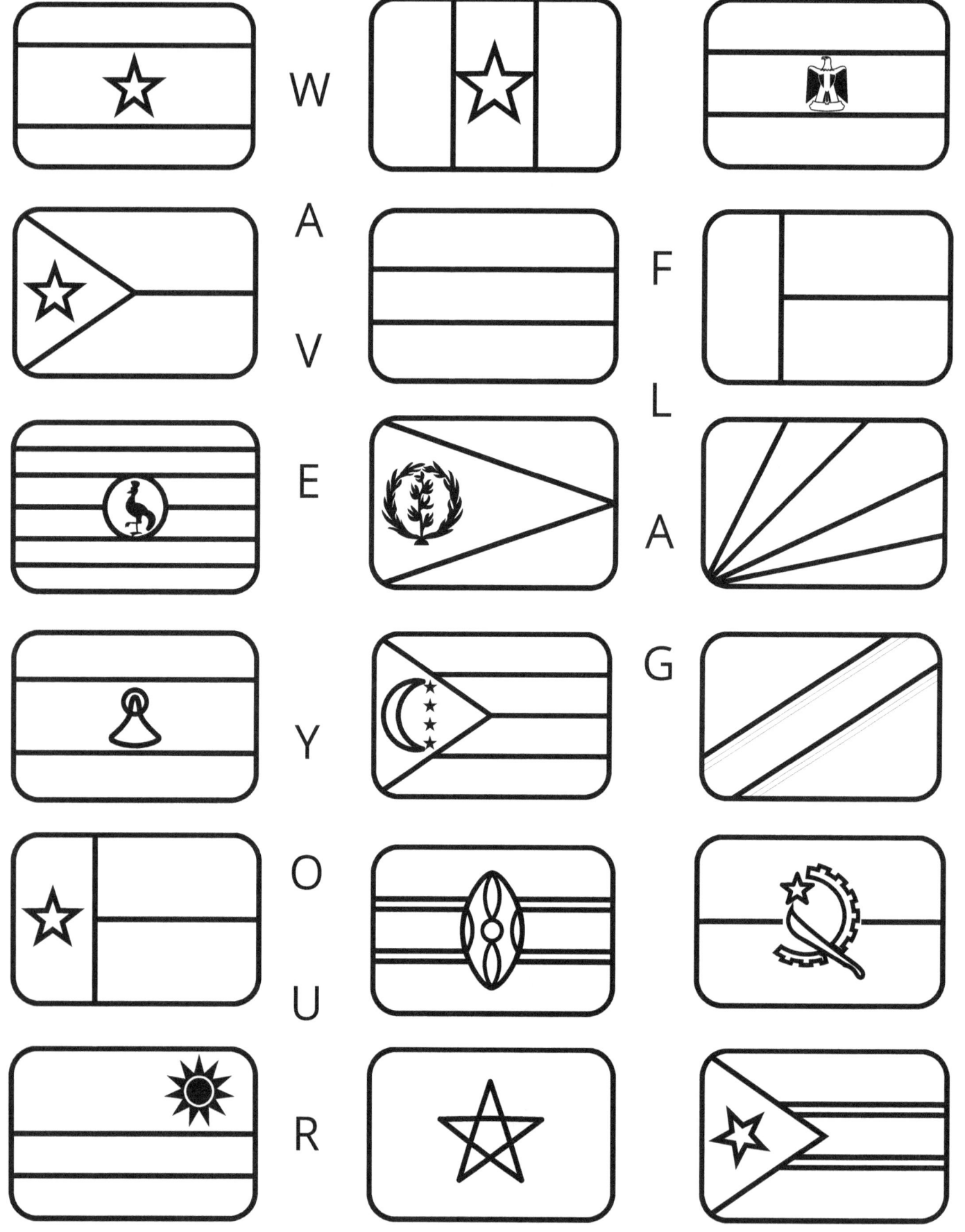

FLAGS OF AFRICA

African Hairstyles

Directions: Identify the braid type by filling in the missing word.

Hair is a source of pride for both Black women and men. Ever wondered where braids originated? The three strand technique started in Africa. Ancient Images have been found at a Nile River burial site called Saqqara. Braids represented status, wealth, religion, age, marital status and more.

This style is also seen in Ancient Africa. It is braided tightly throughout the scalp but starts and ends in a large, thick braid.

_ _ _ _ _ _ O _

They appear in Hieroglyphics and sculpture from 500 BC. This hairstyle is also called banana braids. It starts off small and goes into a larger, thicker braid towards the middle.

_ _ _ _

The Fula tribe is a large nomadic people found in West Africa and Sahel Region. This style is five braids that hang down or loop and has a coiffure in the middle.

_ _ _ _ _ O _

This style can be seen in 3500 BC South Africa. The hair is divided in small plaits and hangs away from the hair. They closely resemble the Embebi braids of Namibia.

_ _ O _

This style dates back to 3000 BC for women & 19th century for men as shown in Ethiopia. This style is braided flat against the scalp and can be straight or curvy lines.

O _ _ _ _ _ _

This is thought to originate in Jamaica but comes from Africa. The Himba people in Namibia achieve this look by using the following ingredients Goat hair, butter and ochre.

_ _ _ _ _ O _ _ _

Embrace your __ __ __ __ __ !

 # African Jewelry

Fill in the blank with the correct letter to complete the sentence.

The oldest form of jewelry was found in the Blombos cave in __out__ A__ri__a.

Jewelry was used to __rad__ and barter for things such as food, cloth and unfortunately even s__a__es.

Mollusk Shells were used as __ea__s and are believed to be __5,000 years old.

Co__rie Shells are an important part of ancient history and symbolize female __erti__ity.

African Jewelry has been made from the following items bones, __eathers, __eeds, i_ory, animal teeth & hair etc.

The African Jewelry is not just ornamental but is worn for __eremonies, r__tuals, statu__ or to convey a message.

A very common practice in Ethiopia involves placing the li__ di__c in a womens mouth before marriage.

In __ali, the Fulan__ women use ___old earrings to display their wealth, the bigger the better shows your family status.

In __airobi, Ken__a, the __urkani tribe women are known to wear large beaded necklaces that can only be taken off if they are ill or mourning.

African Languages

There are between 1,500-2,000 languages in Africa. The language is mostly in oral form and very few are written. They can be broken down into 4 categories.

Niger-Congo/Nilo-Saharan/Afroasiatic/Khoisan

A-1	E-5	I-9	M-13	Q-17	U-21	Y-25
B-2	F-6	J-10	N-14	R-18	V-22	Z-26
C-3	G-7	K-11	O-15	S-19	W-23	
D-4	H-8	L-12	P-16	T-20	X-24	

There are 10 major languages spoken in Africa. Decode them below using the numbers above.

9 7 2 15

_ _ _ _

26 21 12 21

_ _ _ _

19 8 15 14 1

_ _ _ _ _

15 18 15 13 15

_ _ _ _ _

8 1 21 19 1

_ _ _ _ _

1 18 1 2 9 3

_ _ _ _ _ _

6 18 5 14 3 8

_ _ _ _ _ _

25 15 18 21 2 1

_ _ _ _ _ _

1 13 8 1 18 9 3

_ _ _ _ _ _ _

19 23 1 8 9 12 9

_ _ _ _ _ _ _

AFRICAN MUSICAL INSTRUMENTS

PAIR THE WORD TO THE CORRESPONDING MUSICAL INSTRUMENT

KORA
GUIRO
AGOGO
SHEKERE
CASTANETS

DJEMBE
BALAFON
ALGAITA
MARIMBA
MARACAS

UDU
MBIRA
AKOTING
TALKING DRUM
MUSICAL BOW

 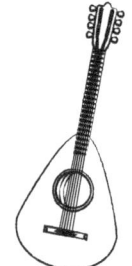  

 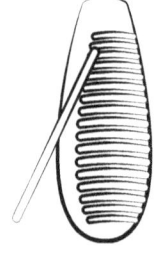  

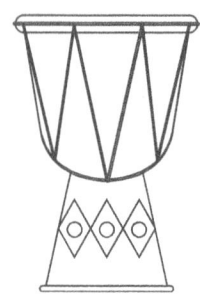  

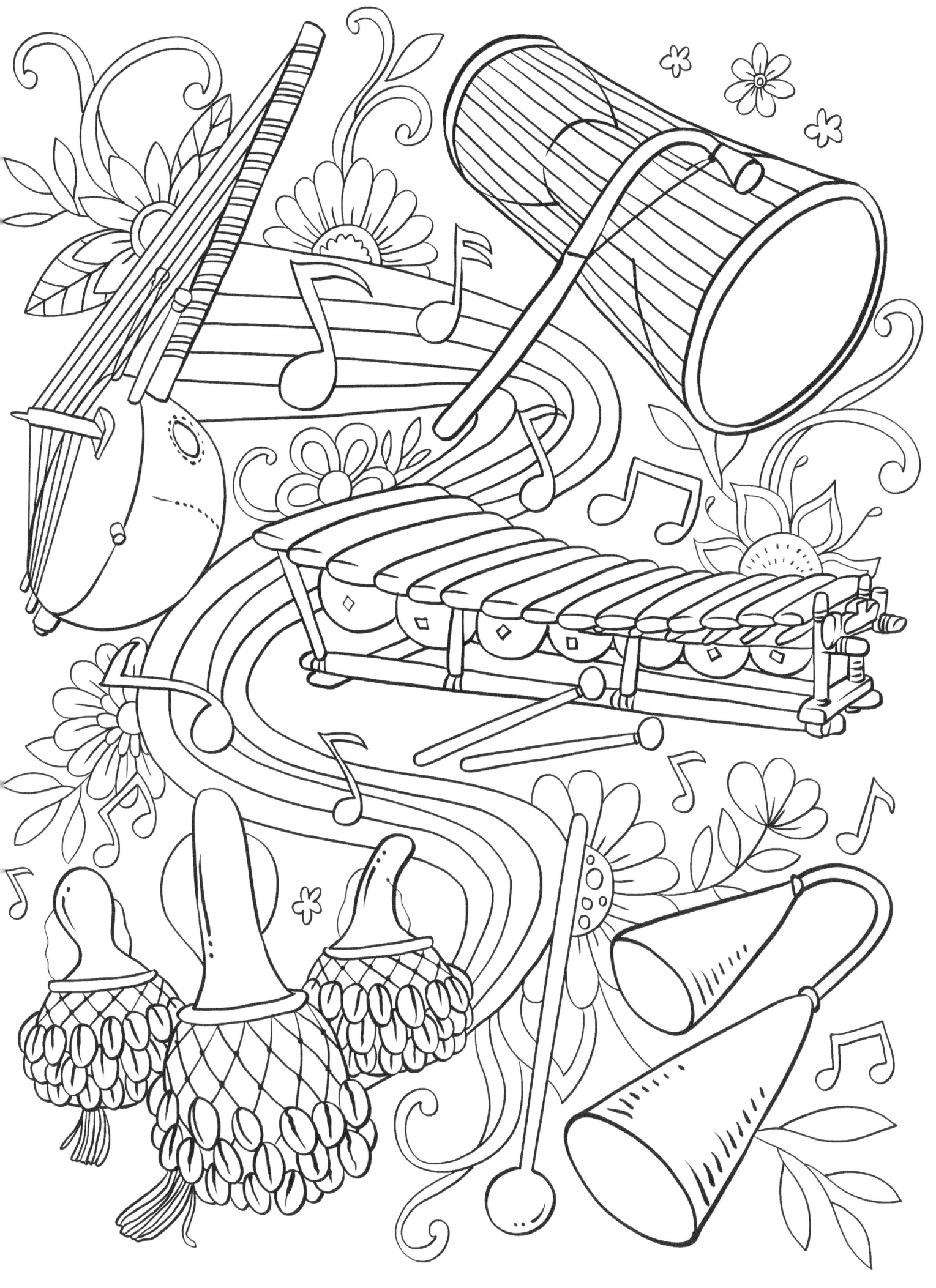

Africa Travel List Challenge

Place a check next to the places you have visited

- ☐ Djenne in Mali
- ☐ Pyramids of Giza
- ☐ Serengeti Safari Park
- ☐ Visit the Maasai Warriors
- ☐ Namibia Skeleton Coast
- ☐ Great Mosque of Djenne
- ☐ Elmina Castles in Ghana
- ☐ Devils Pool, Victoria Falls
- ☐ Rwanda: Gorilla Trekking
- ☐ Morrocco: Sahara Desert
- ☐ Capetown: Table Mountain
- ☐ Swimming in Lake Malawi
- ☐ Botswana: Okavango Delta
- ☐ Tanzania: Climb Kilimanjaro
- ☐ Mauritius, Seven Colored Earths of Chamarel

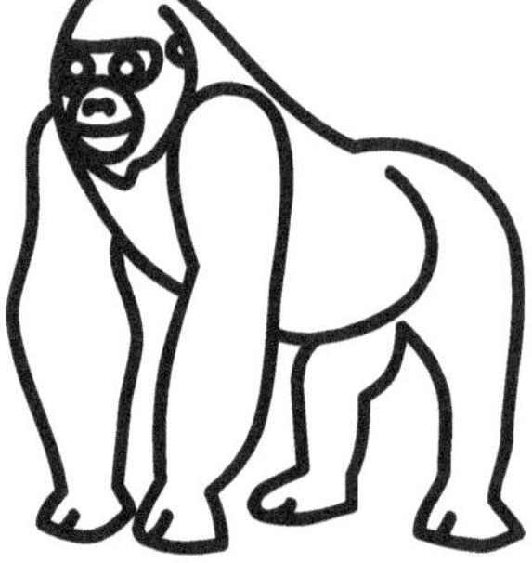

ANGOLA

Match the Angolan food name with the correct ingredients

1. Funge A. Boiled cassava leaves mixed with ground peanuts
2. Kizaca B. Game meat cooked with animal's blood
3. Calulu C. Sour milk made from mucubal cattle
4. Catatos D. Porridge made from cassava flour
5. Cabidela E. Sweet yellow custard or pudding
6. Leite Azedo F. Chicken and red palm oil sauce
7. Cocada Amarela G. Fried caterpillars with garlic
8. Ginguba Torrada H. Stew dried fish & vegetables
9. Muamba de Galinha I. Grasshoppers in red wine
10. Gafanhotos de Palmeira J. Roasted peanuts

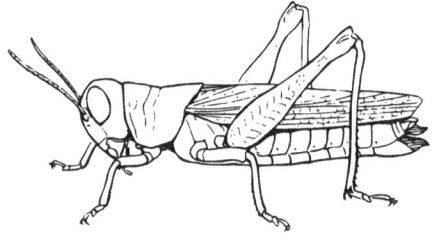

Cameroon

TRUTH

- What is the capital of Cameroon?
- How many countries border Cameroon?
- What drink is Cameroon known for?
- What are the two official languages of Cameroon?
- What is the legal age for marriage for boys and girls?
- When did Cameroon become an independent republic?
- Who was elected in 1984, 1988 & continues to be president?

OR

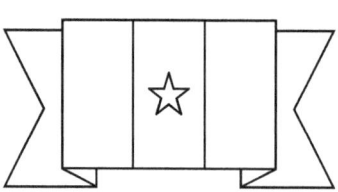

DARE

- Text or call someone & say "I Love You" in French
- Eat a dish with your hands
- Give a Dowry to your opponent
- Dance to a Cameroonian song & post on FB or IG
- Drink a coffee banana smoothie
- Create a song or rap about National Unity
- Make up a 20-second handshake

COMOROS

The words are related to Comoros. Have your partner guess the word at the top of each box written in White. Remember you cannot say the words written in Black when describing the word or you lose a point. 30 seconds on the clock. Now switch partners.

TABOO EDITION — **GROUP ACTIVITY**

VOLCANO	**LOBSTER**	**MOON**
Erupt	Crab	Sun
Lava	Claw	Yellow
Ash	Shrimp	Star
Mountain	Seafood	Crescent
Eruption	Tail	Night

PERFUME	**ARABIC**	**ISLANDS**
Smell	Gum	Virgin
Fragrance	Arab	Isles
Scent	English	Continents
Cologne	Hebrew	Hawaii
Aroma	Numeral	Tropical

ISLAM	**FISHING**	**MARRIAGE**
Religion	Rod	Wedding
Muslim	Net	Divorce
Christianity	Fish	Ring
Judaism	Reel	Love
Hindu	Pole	Wed

| Provide facts about the Afar and Somali people. | What national dish are you eating? |

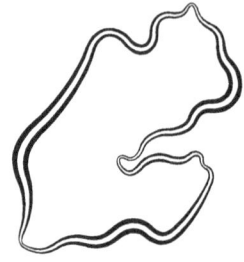 # Djibouti

Research and answer the following questions related to Djibouti

| How is Eid al-Adha celebrated in Djibouti City? | What clothing is worn by women on special occasions? |

Solve Egyptian Hieroglyphics

Longest River in Africa

E

The Capital of Egypt

G

Y

Human Face and body of a lion

P

Last active Pharaoh in Ptolemaic Egypt

T

Greatest Open Air Museum ancient Egyptian temples

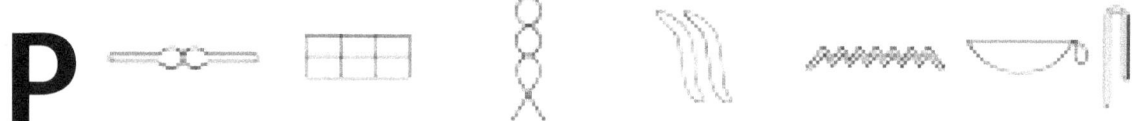

 # ERITREA

USING THE WORDS BELOW RELATED TO ERITREA, CREATE YOUR OWN STORY AND CHARACTERS

CAMEL	ITALY
MUSLIM	DORHO
ARABIC	NAKFA
ASMARA	INJERA
TIGRENYA	KORUNKA
RED OF SEA	CONFLICT
SALT MINING	FOOTBALL
HORN OF AFRICA	INDEPENDENCE

Ethiopia

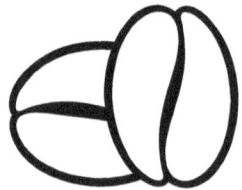
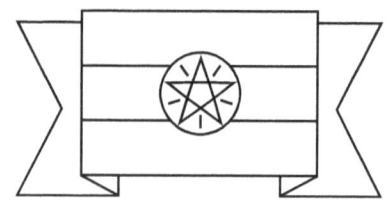

The scoop on Ethiopia. Decode the messages to find interesting facts about the beautiful country.

Although many people believe that this started in Jamaica, Ethiopia is the spiritual birthplace of the _____ Movement

R _ _ _ _ _ _ _ _ A _ _ _ I

Ethiopia is the highest producer of ------ in Africa. This drink was discovered by a goat herder named Kaldi

_ _ _ F _ _ E _

This flat spongy cuisine is usually topped with vegetables and stews

_ _ _ J E _ _ _

_____ Selassie I was the last Ethiopian emperor

_ _ A _ _ _ _

The Ethiopian calendar has 13 months in a year and is called ----

_ _ _ _ Z

Did You Know?

Ethiopia is the only independent country and has never been colonized. Lucy, a 3.2 million year old hominid skeleton was found in Hadar, Ethiopia. Time is different, sunrise starts at 1pm and sunset is 12pm. The word Ethiopia is mentioned at least 45x in the Bible and is noted in the Quran as well as other books.

Gabon
MASK & FOLKLORE

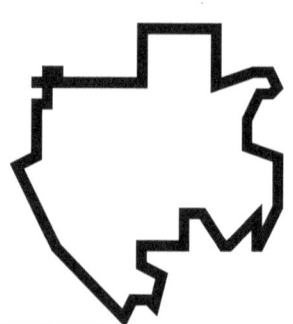

1

Masks are used in ceremonies such as birth, life and death.

Draw it in the box here.

2

The Gabonese used oral tradition to create folklore that passes down from generation to generation.

Create a folklore tale below of something that you would like to tell your future grandchildren.

GHANA

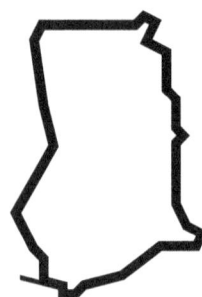
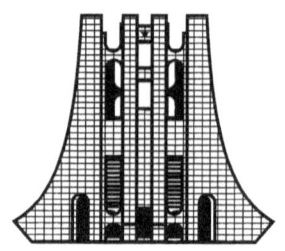

```
K E C O V F S C F F L X I U L U V S W U
W C A M A Q P X K I Q D Y R B Q L K A Q
A I P K A K U M N A T I O N A L P A R K
M R E I A Q G V X P A N E N A Y B B C C
E F C K K N M R E C E L A F G L K A C B
N O O E E E F I A M A R H A W V A A F
K L A N B D J R W I Y E N C S Q T W T C
R L S K R K F E N H T I K U V A W K T F
U O T E L A M A T A C S T E T Z I A W C
M J D Y T P C P W I T A S K T S G D W Z
A O I S E A Y O M A A L E J U V O S J T
H H E N S N P X R H L M F B Q M X U P H
I W O T X M E N I W M L A P I V A J P E
M Y L K A F U F U B N A P R F D N S S Y
K E U T X R W U A V Z D N E K E A A I T
G I N E W T M O S O B E K A L E A B R E
X I T D L N Y O J N A M K A H D T O A H
K H H J F C D A Y F F V H U E G C K B L
K E N T E C L O T H S C Q M H G B E C O
A S H U E G C H A Q S A N K O F A K N H
```

ACCRA	JOLLOF RICE	
AKAN	KAKUM NATIONAL PARK	KINTAMPO WATERFALLS
AKWAABA	KEJETIA MARKET	KUMASI
ASHANTI	KENKEY	KWAME NKRUMAH
BLACK STAR	KENTE CLOTH	LABADI BEACH
CAPECOAST	SANKOFA	LAKE BOSOMTWE
CHALE	TAMALE	MEDAASE
ELMINA CASTLE	TRO	PALM WINE
FUFU	TWI	PEANUT SOUP
GHANA	WEST AFRICA	REDRED

Guinea Bissau

Group Scavenger Hunt: Be the first person to complete all activities.

Google a Photo of Amilcar Cabral

Find Cashews and eat 2

Describe the Guinea Bissau flag

Find the international dialing code

State the motto of the country 3x

Show recipe for Abacate Com Tuna

Say Hello My Name is _____ in Portugese

Search for Gumbe music and play it for 2 minutes

Retrieve 3 of your favorite photos of the Guinea Bissau Carnival

KENYA
MAASAI CULTURE & TRADITIONS

NEVER HAVE I EVER INSTRUCTIONS:

Get a drink of your choice and read each bullet point. If you've **not** done that bullet point item, you must take a drink. If you **have** done the bullet point item, you are safe from taking a drink!

- SPEAK SWAHILI
- TRAVELED TO KENYA
- EVER BEEN CIRCUMCISED
- DRANK COWS OR GOAT BLOOD
- KILLED A LION USING A SPEAR
- KNOW OF SOMEONE WHO HAD A PREDATOR BURIAL
- BUILT A HUT USING WOOD, COW DUNG, GRASS AND STICKS
- LIVED A NOMADIC LIFE; SURVIVING OFF HERDING CATTLE & GOATS
- INHERITED WEALTH FROM YOUR FATHER AND SHARED IT WITH YOUR ELDEST SIBLING
- JUMPED IN THE AIR WHILE MAKING SOUNDS TO ATTRACT SOMEONE OF THE OPPOSITE SEX

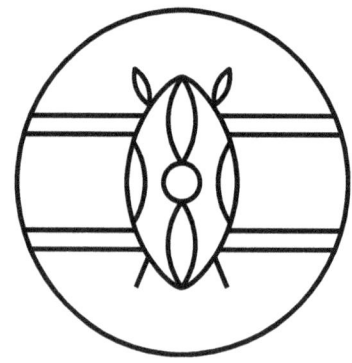

Lesotho

2 TRUTHS AND 1 LIE
CIRCLE WHICH STATEMENT IS A LIE

1. Black Panther Marvel Movie had aspects of Lesotho:
   a. Wkabi wore a Lesotho-inspired blanket
   b. Lesotho people in the movie rode on horses
   c. The Border Tribe were warriors disguised as farmers

2. Lesotho national language:
   a. Sesotho
   b. Swahili
   c. English

3. What currency is accepted in Lesotho:
   a. Ghana Cedis
   b. South African Rand
   c. Lesotho Loti

4. Basotho blanket is worn for:
   a. Birth, Death & Marriage
   b. Cultural identification
   c. Used to protect animals from the cold

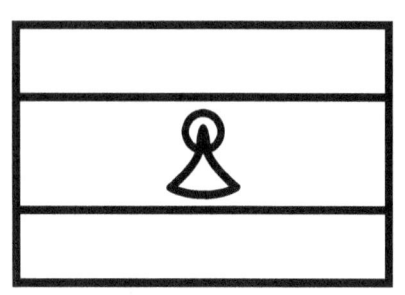

5. Basotho Hat aka Mokorotlo is made from:
   a. Cotton
   b. Straw
   c. Shape of mountains in the country

Liberia

Migration from America to Africa

In 1821, the American Colonization Society created Liberia for freed slaves. A freed man from Virginia named Joseph Jenkin Roberts became the first governor in 1841. On July 26, 1847 Liberia had declared its independence. By 1867 over 10,000 African Americans migrated to Africa and were known as Americo-Liberians. Liberia was involved in 2 civil wars from 1989-2003.

Influential Leaders

In 2005, Ellen Johnson Sirleaf became the first female president of Liberia. In 2011 she was awarded The Nobel Peace Prize for her peace efforts and women's rights.

Questions & Answers

Why was Liberia created?

Who was Mr. Joseph Roberts?

What year did Liberia declare independence?

Would you migrate to Africa after being freed in America?

Leymah Gbowee is a social worker and a women's rights activist. She is known for bringing together Christian and Muslim women for a peaceful movement that would play a important role in ending the civil war. Leymah is the founder of an organization called Gbowee Peace Foundation Africa

The Scoop about Liberia

Currency: Liberian Dollar
16 recognized ethnic groups
Polygamy is widely practised
English is the official language
Dumboy (cassava) is the national dish
Monrovia is the capital named after President James Monroe

Richelieu Dennis came to America after leaving Liberia due to the Civil War. He went to business school and soon after created a skin care line. With his mother he co-founded Sundial, a natural bath and body care products. In 2018, he also purchased Essence Magazine.

Secret Code

Use the alphabet secret code to find Liberia's Motto "The ____ __ ____ Brought us Here"

12 15 22 5   15 6   12 9 2 5 18 20 25

__ __ __ __   __ __   __ __ __ __ __ __

Madagascar

Fill in the blank using the words bank below

Lemur	Lamba	Africa
Indian	Baobab	French
Periwinkle	Malagasy	Moraingy

1. Madagascar was once a _____ colony.

2. _____ is a form of bare-fisted combat sport.

3. The _____ tree is known as the Tree of Life.

4. Madagascar is located in the _____ Ocean.

5. _____ is the traditional garment worn by islanders.

6. There are over 100 species of _____ found in Madagascar.

7. The official languages of Madagascar are French and _____.

8. Name of the movie Madagascar 2: Escape to _____.

9. The Madagascar _____ flower is used for medicinal purposes.

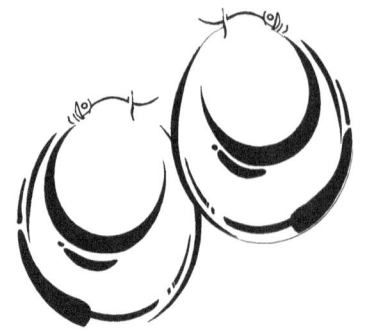  

Provide 7 additional interesting facts about Mali

1. Mali is a landlocked country surrounded by Senegal, Burkina Faso, Niger, Ivory Coast, Algeria, Guinea and Mauritania.

2. In 1907, The Great Mosque of Djenne was constructed as the world's largest mud-brick building.

3. Fulani women wear kwottone kanye (gold earrings) as a sign of wealth.

4.

5.

6.

7.

8.

9.

10.

Morocco Edition

This   Or   That

Circle

This	That
Cook with Saffron	Eat Cumin on Hummus
Watch Cleopatra Movie	Watch Game of Thrones
Visit Chefchaouen	Take a tour of Casablanca
Speak French Fluently	Learn to Speak Arabic
Eat Chicken Bastilla	Devour Lamb Tagine
Rap with French Montana	Meet Jean Reno
Purchase a Morrocan Lamp	Buy a Moroccan Rug
Ride a Camel	Go Horseback Riding
Visit the Sahara Desert	Climb Atlas Mountains
Shop in Marrakech Medina	Shop at Fes Tannery

Namibia
If the Himba Tribe had Twitter

Himba is an ethnic group living in Northern Namibia of Kunene Region aka Kaokaland. The tribe live according to ancient tradition and are semi-nomadic hunter gatherers. They speak Otjihimba, a dialect of the Herero language. In the Himba culture they have a double lineage (matriarchal and patriarchal) which means they rely on multiple clans. The women are often topless and wear skirts made of goat skinned cloth and men wear loin cloth and sandals for foot wear made of old car tires.

Below are fictional Tweets from the Himba Tribe. Use the clues to learn more about their lifestyle.

1. @serialdater I have a non-traditional relationship. Monday thru Thursday, I'm with Mariann. On the weekend, I wine and dine with Rose #livingmybestlife #spouse #sisterwives

    Identify the type of relationship.

2. @ancestrydna It is Sunday but, you will not find me in church. For spiritual guidance, I communicate daily with my family lineage. They have paved the road for myself & future generations. #forefathers #heknowsmyheart

    Who does the Himba Worship?

3. @brunchandmimosas This brunch is lit, the DJ is banging and, my food is the bomb. I know it's controversial but, I prefer eating this dish topped with sugar, butter instead of salt and pepper. #foodie #teamsugarnosalt

    What do the Himba people eat daily?

4. @partyanimal It is my birthday weekend! My beaded ankle bracelets are cute and match my skirt but, I also wear them to protect my skin. #snakes #critters #imscared

    Women wear ankle bracelets to protect their skin from what?

5. @overworkedandunderpaid I have been working hard all day and can't wait to bathe when I get home. People get high from the fumes but, this is how I clean my melanated body #420 #sofreshandsoclean

    How do the Himba women bathe?

6. @brownskingirl My granny told me that I should never walk out of the house with ashy skin. As an entrepreneur, I created a new skincare line. The cream consists of Hematite stone, butter & smoke. #supportblackbusiness

    What is the name of this new product line?

7. @manofthehouse I am the head of the household. I refuse to carry water to the village or build a home but, I will advise the community on various issues. #justice #criminalsystem #foreignaffairs

    Men provide advice on what type of matters?

NIGERIA BINGO

PLACE AN X IN THE SQUARE FOR EACH ACTIVITY COMPLETED

WEAR A GELE	COOK JOLLOF RICE	WATCH SUPER EAGLES PLAY FOOTBALL	CELEBRATE NIGERIAN INDEPENDENCE DAY	VISITED IGBOLAND
PARTICIPATE IN RAMADAN	WATCH NOLLYWOOD MOVIES	LISTEN TO FELA KUTI	VISITED AT LEAST 10 STATES	ATTEND CHURCH ON CHRISTMAS
EVER SUNG OR DANCED TO DAVIDO	SHOP AT UTAKO MARKET	NIGERIA	WORN TRADITIONAL CLOTHING	ATTENDED A DOUBLE WEDDING CEREMONY
VISITED ZUMA ROCK	SPEAK HAUSA	ARRIVED ON AFRICAN TIME	WAVE A NIGERIAN FLAG	EATEN MOI MOI AS A SNACK
KNOW YORUBA TWINS	EAT EGUSI SOUP	SHAKE WITH RIGHT HAND	HAVE BEEN SPRAYED WITH NAIRA	SAID THE WORD EHEN OR AMEBO

 # RWANDA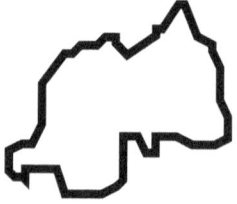

Kigali is the cleanest city in Africa. Rwanda has banned the use of plastic bags and has a community wide event where they clean the city once a month. If you were given a $50,000 grant to sanitize your city, how would you use the money and involve the community?

After the genocide, the population of women increased. In 2003, President Kagame declared that 30% of parliament positions should be held by women. If you could run for any political office, which would you choose and why? How can we continue to ensure and improve gender equality around the world?

Rwanda is a peaceful country. Of all the African nations, Rwanda ranks #3 as the least corrupt city. In 2001, Rwanda introduced Gacaca Court, A community based justice system. It's a system where community members testify freely, without lawyers, and cases are decided by a panel of judges. You create the outline for a justice program that would be equitable and equal for all community members.

The government created the Rwanda Development Board allowing people from around the world to invest in business opportunities. It only takes two days to register your business. If you could invest a business in Rwanda what would it be and why?

I SPY Senegal

Search and Color! How many similar photos can you find?

2 flags, 2 Wrestlers, 3 lakes, 3 Rice, 4 seashells, 4 Baobab Trees, 5 fish, 5 Peanuts, 6 Muslim representation 6 Sheep, 7 birds

 # Seychelles

Seychelles is known as paradise on earth. It has deep blue water, sandy shores and has rare bird species.

Close your eyes, imagine the scenery and complete the poem:

> Rays of sunshine penetrate my melanin skin
> Vibrations of the waves crashing swiftly
> Powdery sand beneath my feet
> Noise of the pure white tern flying above
> Soothing thoughts of peacefulness

SIERRA LEONE

UNSCRAMBLE THE WORDS USING THE CLUES BELOW

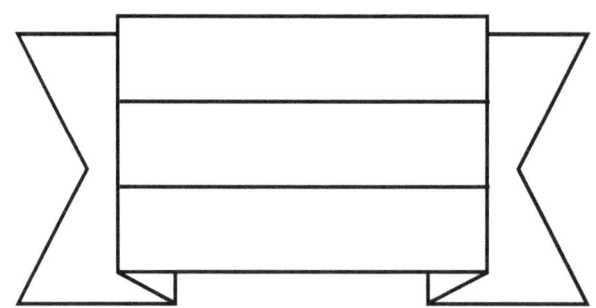

ETHNIC GROUP
ENEDM

HIGHEST PEAK
NOTUM TUAMIBNIN

COUNTRY NATIONAL DISH
AASACVS VEAELS

CAPITAL AND LARGEST CITY
TOREWENF

ENGLIGH BASED CREOLE SPOKEN
RIKO

A MINERAL FOUND IN SIERRA LEONE
UAXTIBE

THIS CONFLICT OCCURRED BETWEEN 1991-2002
IAERSR EOLEN VLCII RWA

FREEDOM FROM SLAVERY & PRAYER TO ANCESTORS
TTNOCO RETE

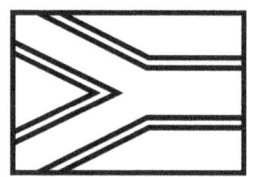 # South Africa

APARTHEID

FROM 1948 UNTIL THE EARLY 1990S APARTHEID EXISTED IN SOUTH AFRICA. APARTHEID WAS A LAW THAT WOULD KEEP NON- WHITE CITIZENS SEGREGATED IN EVERY ASPECT OF DAILY LIFE.

MATCH THE YEAR TO THE CORRECT STATEMENT TO CREATE A TIMELINE.

1913

1948

1950

1959

1963

1975

1976

1990

1994

THE UN SECURITY COUNCIL VOTED TO IMPOSE A MANDATORY EMBARGO ON THE SALE OF ARMS TO SOUTH AFRICA.

NELSON MANDELA, FOUNDER OF UMKHONTO WE SIZWE "SPEAR OF NATION" WAS IMPRISONED FOR BEING AN ACTIVIST IN THE APARTHEID MOVEMENT.

THE PROMOTION OF BANTU SELF-GOVERNMENT ACT CREATED 10 BANTU HOMELANDS KNOWN AS BANTUSTANS. SEPARATION CAUSED THE GOVERNMENT TO CLAIM THAT THERE WAS NO BLACK MAJORITY AND PREVENTED THEM FROM FORMING A NATIONAL ORGANIZATION.

THE LAND ACT WAS PASSED, IT BECAME ILLEGAL FOR BLACK AFRICANS TO BUY, LEASE OR LIVE ON LAND OUTSIDE OF "RESERVES." IT ALSO PROHIBITED THE SALE OF LAND BETWEEN WHITE AND BLACK AFRICANS.

F.W DE KLERK GOVERNMENT REPEALED LAWS SUCH AS THE PRA, INTERACIAL SEX AND MARRAIGE AND FREED MANDELA ON FEBRAURY.

BLACK STUDENTS IN SOWETO PROTESTED AGAINST BLACK STUDENTS' REQUIREMENT TO SPEAK AFRIKAANS. THE POLICE OPENED GUN FIRE AND THREW TEAR GAS. THIS BROUGHT NATIONAL ATTENTION TO S.A.

ON MAY 10 MANDELA WAS INAUGURATED AS THE FIRST DEMOCRATIC PRESIDENT.

THE AFRIKANER NATIONAL PARTY WON UNDER THE POLITICAL SLOGAN "APARTHEID" WHICH MEANS APARTNESS.

THE POPULATION REGISTRATION ACT (PRA) SEPARATED SOUTH AFRICAN RACE INTO THE FOLLOWING CATEGORIES: WHITE, COLORED (MIXED RACE) AND BANTU (BLACK AFRICANS).

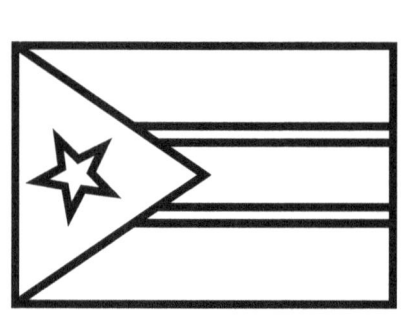# SOUTH SUDAN

How many words can you make from the word South Sudan?

1.
2.
3.
4.
5.
6.
7.
8.
9.
10.
11.
12.
13.
14.
15.
16.
17.
18.
19.
20.

TRUE (T) OR FALSE (F)

Tanzania is surrounded by 4 countries __
The Tanzania flag is green, red, black and yellow __
The use of your left hand is seen as impolite __
The official language is Swahili __

CIRCLE THE CORRECT ANSWER

What is the capital of Zanzibar?
a. Stone Town
b. Zanzibar City
c. Dar Es Salaam

What is the most prominent religion in Zanzibar?
a. Christian
b. Catholic
c. Islam

What spices is Zanzibar known for?
a. Cloves, nutmeg, cinnamon and black pepper
b. Black pepper, cinnamon, lemon pepper and salt
c. Cinnamon, cloves, coriander and cumin

FILL IN THE BLANK

_____ happens when this animal crosses the Serengeti from the Mara River.

_____ is where there is the earliest evidence of humans, leading scientists to believe humans originated in Africa.

UGANDA

DOWN
1. UGANDA'S LARGEST EXPORT
3. THIS CRANE IS THE NATIONAL BIRD
5. SECOND LARGEST LAKE
6. FOREIGNERS ARE CALLED
7. UGANDA'S LARGEST CITY
8. NATIONAL CULTURAL DRESS
11. TALLEST MOUNTAIN RANGE
12. OFFICIAL LANGUAGE

ACROSS
2. NATIONAL ANIMAL
4. LINE DIVIDING THE NORTH AND SOUTH
6. NATIONAL DISH
9. FALLS IN NATIONAL PARK
10. REPRESENTS DEFENDING THE COUNTRY
12. LOCAL CURRENCY
13. MOST COMMON INSTRUMENT
14. LARGEST ETHNIC GROUP
15. OMELETTE WRAPPED IN CHAPATI

WODAABE

The nomadic Wodaabe are a small subgroup of the Fulani ethnic people. They primarily live in the deserts of Chad, Niger, Cameroon, Nigeria and Central Republic of Africa. Wodaabe are considered to be the vainest people in the world and physical beauty is very important. They adorn themselves with tattoos, body paint, colorful sashes and jewels. At the end of the rainy season, they have the Gerwewol ceremony,. It is a week-long courtship ceremony in which the men wear makeup, jewelry and show off their white teeth in order to attract a woman to marry and to be crowned the most beautiful.

Activity: Let's pretend the Wodaabe now have access to technology and have discovered a dating app called Taboo Connection. Create a dating profile bio below that would entice a Wodaabe to connect with you.

Name:

Age:

Location:

Favorite Food:

Most memorable lesson:

Places you love to Travel:

Who do you cherish the most?

What songs makes you dance?

What are your non negotiables?

What has been your proudest moment?

What are you looking for in a potential mate?

Tiffany travels to the Motherland

My name is Tiffany. While attending college, I always had a desire to visit Africa. During my Junior year, I signed up for a six week summer study abroad to Ghana. I fell in love with the country and continue to visit every couple of years. My proudest moment was organizing and hosting a small group trip to Ghana for the Year of the Return.

As a graduate student and Student Council President at Howard University, I had the opportunity to visit South Africa. While there, I shadowed other social work professionals and volunteered at community organizations.

For leisure, I visited Morocco. My most memorable moments were watching the stars in the Sahara desert, eating lamb tagine and having a photoshoot in the blue city known as Chefchouen.

In 2009, I briefly visited Burkina Faso. My funniest memory was attempting to order a hamburger in English and the staff only spoke French.

After doing a family DNA test, I was happy to learn that I am from Sierra Leone and Guinea Bissau. My goal is to visit all 54 countries in Africa.

Write FA or FI next to each statement below

F A C T

Rode a camel in the Sahara Desert ___
Vacationed in Morocco with my family ___
Visited Nelson Mandela jail cell in Capetown ___
Traveled to Burkina Faso by car, van, and boat ___
First international trip was to Ghana West Africa ___
Went to Johannesburg, SA with Howard University __
Dream Africa trip is to Seychelles to relax on the beach __
Lived in Ghana for 2 months & volunteered at a school __

F I C T I O N

EXPAT JOURNEY

LET'S PRETEND, YOU ARE MOVING TO AFRICA AS AN EXPAT! AN EXPAT IS SOMEONE WHO LIVES OUTSIDE OF THEIR HOME COUNTRY. DECIDE WHICH COUNTRY YOU WILL BE LIVING IN? WHAT TYPES OF THINGS WILL YOU PACK? DRAW OR WRITE THE ITEMS YOU WILL INCLUDE IN YOUR SUITCASE.

JOURNEY TO AFRICA MAZE

Catch a flight and not feelings!
Find your way to your new home in the motherland.
You will be welcomed with open arms.

WELCOME HOME

Reflections

What did **you** learn?

What did **you** already know about Africa?

Where have **you** been in Africa?

What countries do **you** want to visit in Africa?

Favorite coloring page/ activity

PLANNING A TRIP TO AFRICA

IF YOU ARE INTERESTED IN TAKING A TRIP TO AFRICA, LET'S HELP YOU PLAN THE VACATION OF YOUR DREAMS
CONTACT:
EMAIL: SWEETTIFFYSINSPIRATIONS@GMAIL.COM
WEBSITE: WWW.HUESOFAFRICA.COM
INSTAGRAM: @HUES_OF_AFRICA

Answer Key

Truth About Africa
Countries, Continent, Islam, Ethiopia, Nile, Diamonds, Timbuktu, Liberia, Hippos, Arabic, Fossils

African Cuisine
S1: South Africa (S) S2: East Africa (E) S3: North Africa (N) S4: West Africa (W)

African Fabric
1C, 2A, 3D, 4B

African Flags
Column 1: Ghana, Djibouti, Uganda, Lesotho, Guinea Bissau, Rwanda
Column 2: Cameron, Sierra Leone, Eritrea, Comoros, Kenya, Morocco
Column 3: Egypt, Madagascar, Seychelles, Tanzania, Angola, South Sudan

African Hairstyles
Goddess, Ghana, Fulani, Box, Cornrows, Dreadlocks, Coils

Africa Jewelry
1) South Africa, 2) Trade, Slaves, 3) Beads, 75,000, 4) Cowrie, Fertility
5) Feathers, Seeds, Ivory 6) Ceremonies, Rituals, Status 7) Lip Disc
8) Mali, Fulani, Gold 9) Nairobi, Kenya, Turkani

African Languages
Column 1: Igbo, Zulu, Shona, Oromo, Hausa
Column 2: Arabic, French, Yoruba, Amharic, Swahili

African Musical Instruments
Column 1: Algaita, Udu, Balafon, Djembe
Column 2: Kora, Maracas, Guiro, Castanets
Column 3: Musical Bow, Shekere, Mbira, Talking Drum
Column 4: Akoting, Marimba, Agogo

Angola
1D, 2A, 3H, 4G, 5B, 6C, 7E, 8J, 9F, 10I

Cameroon
Yaounde, 6, Coffee, English & French, Boys 18 y/o & Girls 15 y/o, January 1, 1960, Paul Biya

Answer Key

Egypt
Nile, Cairo, Sphinx, Cleopatra, Luxor

Ethiopia
Rastafari, Coffee, Injera, Haile, Ge'ez

Lesotho
1B, 2B, 3A, 4C, 5A

Liberia
Created for freed slaves, Roberts was the first governor of Liberia, July 26, 1847
Secret Code: Love of Liberty

Madagascar
French, Moraingy, Baobab, Indian, Lamba, Lemur, Malagasy, Africa, Periwinkle

Namibia
Polygamy, Ancestors, Grits aka Porridge, Venomous Animal Bites, Herbs and Smoke, Red Ochre, Legal Trials and or Political

Sierra Leone
Mende, Mount Bintumani, Cassava Leaves, Freetown,
Krio, Bauxite, Sierra Leone Civil War, Cotton Tree

South Africa
Column 1: 1976, 1913, 1975, 1948
Column 2: 1963, 1959, 1990, 1994, 1950

South Sudan
Hat, Sun, Hot, Dan, Hand, Not, Out, Suds, Ton, Has,
And, Dots, Stud, Don't, Tod, Hut, Nod, Don, Dust, Toss

Tanzania
True, False, False, True
B, C, A
Wildebeest Migration. Olduvai Gorge

Uganda
Across: Kob, Equator, Matoke, Murchison, Spears, Shilling, Drum, Baganda, Rolex
Down: Coffee, Crested, Victoria, Mzungu, Kampala, Gomesi, Rwenzori, Swahili

Tiffany Travels to the Motherland
FA, FI, FA, FA, FA, FI, FI, FA

www.ingramcontent.com/pod-product-compliance
Lightning Source LLC
Chambersburg PA
CBHW081420080526
44589CB00016B/2608